BROADWAY FOR
BEGINNERS

BROADWAY FOR BEGINNERS

A TOURIST'S GUIDE TO BROADWAY AND OFF-BROADWAY IN NEW YORK CITY

BRIAN GUY

PREVIEW NIGHT PRESS

eBook ISBN 979-8-9942273-2-9
Paperback ISBN 979-8-9942273-0-5
Hardcover ISBN 979-8-9942273-1-2
Large Print Edition ISBN 979-8-9942273-5-0

Published by Preview Night Press
Bainbridge Island, Washington

26021801

This book is dedicated to my autistic son, Anthony, who is the happiest person I know. Anthony has the best attitude of anyone, and he brightens the day of everyone he encounters. I have learned so much from Anthony, and I am one of dozens of people he has changed for the better.

CONTENTS

Acknowledgments   ix

1. CURTAIN SPEECH   1
2. WHY SEE A SHOW ON BROADWAY (OR OFF-
   BROADWAY)?   3
3. WHY DO YOU NEED THIS BOOK?   7
4. TERMINOLOGY   10
5. ACCESSIBILITY   19
6. PICKING A SHOW   21

7. PICKING YOUR SEAT AND BUYING A TICKET   25
   Picking Your Seat   26
   The Cheap Seats   33
   When to Buy   35
   Rush and Lottery Tickets   36
   Sold Out Shows   38
   Performer Alerts   39
   Show Research   39
   Refunds and Exchanges   40

8. WHERE TO STAY   42
9. HOW TO DRESS   44

10. DAY OF THE SHOW   46
    When to Arrive   47
    Food and Beverage Considerations   49
    Where to Eat Before the Show   49
    Subway vs. Ride Share vs. Taxi   50

11. AT THE SHOW   52
    Restrooms   52
    Your Program   53
    Etiquette   54
    Running Late   58

12. INTERMISSION RESTROOM STRATEGY   59

13. AFTER THE SHOW 62
    Stage Door 62

14. CLOSING 65

About the Author 67
Also by Brian Guy 69
Preview Night Press 71

ACKNOWLEDGMENTS

Thank you to all the artists who create live theatre. You make the world a better place. You have allowed me to laugh, cry, learn, feel all the feels, and make new friends. I have recently decided the shows are actually secondary, and it's the people—the theatre people—who make this passion of mine so rewarding.

Thank you so much also to you, the reader, for buying this book and for spending your precious time reading it. I hope you find the stories and tips helpful.

Last but not least, thank you to my friends and family who encouraged me, patiently listened to my latest Broadway stories, and who provided feedback on early drafts of this book. Specifically, thank you to my mom, Lori Batchelder, and to my children Carson Guy, Anthony Guy, and Vivian Guy. Hugs and treats to my dog, Roxie Eponine, who somehow still has more Instagram followers than I do.

1

CURTAIN SPEECH

Welcome to *Broadway for Beginners: A Tourist's Guide to Broadway and Off-Broadway in New York City!* The goal of this book is to tell you everything you need to know to have a successful Broadway experience. What show should you see? Where should you sit? How should you buy your tickets? How do you not get scammed? How should you dress? What is the etiquette during the show? And more.

As of this writing, I have seen over eighty shows this year. Most recently, I saw a record fourteen shows over seven days, including one three-show day. On the flip side, the record low trip involved determining which two shows to see in one day during a quick weekend trip to New York. Whether one show or fourteen shows in a trip, there are always more shows you want to see than there are precious slots available in your schedule (or dollars in your wallet). This book will help you figure it all out and optimize your schedule, your seat, and your budget.

I do not know if you plan to see one show or many shows, and I do not know if you will go by yourself (which is very common) or with others, so my advice will apply to all of these scenarios. No matter what, there will likely be more shows you want to see than you are able to see, so I will offer you advice on how to prioritize what to see now versus during a future trip. When my recommendation is different depending on whether you are by yourself or with others, then I will clarify. For simplicity, I will use the singular words show, ticket, and seat, assuming you are buying one ticket to one show, but know my advice also applies with multiple tickets for multiple seats at multiple shows.

A goal with this book is to help you no matter your budget. If you have a larger budget, this book can help you learn how to get the best seats possible. If you have a "normal person" budget, then this book can help you with strategies to get the best value while avoiding scams.

Check out previewnightpress.com for new Broadway-themed books.

2

WHY SEE A SHOW ON BROADWAY
(OR OFF-BROADWAY)?

B ig Broadway shows may come to your hometown, and
you can sometimes even see them on TV, so why
spend all this money? First, let's address why to see a
live show in the first place, and second, let's explain why it will
likely be so much better in New York City than in your
hometown.

When you see a show live, every single performance is
different, even if only slightly. The goal might be for it to be the
same, but actors are human and do not act 100% the same way
each show. Subtle differences can then influence how that
actor's scene partner responds. A good actor is not delivering
memorized lines and memorized behaviors but is rather
reacting and responding to the other characters and what is
happening around them, so if one character is behaving just
slightly differently, then that can influence the other actor's
feelings and how that actor responds. Even the most minor
nuances can change how you experience the show. This is one
reason it is fun to see a show more than once.

Also, sometimes things go wrong, and actors may need to

improvise a bit to keep the scene on track. For example, if one actor forgets a line, another actor might cover it. With skilled actors, you likely will not even realize any of this is happening. None of this happens in a perfectly edited film, so live theatre is just more exciting. Also, with live theatre, you can look wherever you want to, whereas with film, you are forced to look at whatever the camera is zoomed in on. The next time you go to a live show you have seen before, don't watch the actor who is speaking, and instead, check out what the other actors are doing. What are ensemble members doing? What are actors on stage but not the center of attention doing? In a Broadway show, you will find these other actors are also always acting, 100% of the time, because they are well-trained actors. It can be very fun to watch what everyone else is doing, and it helps you learn more about that character. In film, you aren't allowed to see the reactions of everyone else who is in the scene. The director forces you to watch just one or two faces. You have more control over your own experience in live theatre.

In addition, you have the energy from the audience, which has an impact on the cast. The cast and the audience feed off each other's energy. When I saw *Oh, Mary!* at the very first performance after Cole Escola's Tony Award win the night before (and perhaps Cole stayed up late celebrating?), the cast was clearly exhausted at that Monday night performance (to be clear, the performances were still excellent, and the Tony Awards weekend is indeed exhausting for all), Cole and other cast members told me after the show they did in fact get through that performance thanks to all the energy from the audience.

Similarly, I saw Audra McDonald in *Gypsy* on the Saturday evening before the Tony Awards, and the audience energy was so extreme that Audra gave the performance of a lifetime—far superior, in my opinion, to her out-of-context performance the next night at The Tony Awards, perhaps partially because a Tony Awards audience just isn't as exciting as the live show audience on Tony Eve. That audience made *Gypsy* run for over three hours that night, due to so many interruptions with standing ovations. You don't get this experience at home or even in a movie theater. An analogy would be why people still like to attend live sports events even when the games are aired on TV. The energy from the crowd is so exciting.

Next, let's explain why New York is better (no offense to other cities). The reality is the top talent moves to New York City. It is as simple as this. And I am not talking just about singers and actors, but also your best directors, best scenic designers, best lighting designers, best sound designers, best choreographers—they are all in New York City (and perhaps London). Now add in the fact that the venues are smaller and more intimate, and you can create a set and lighting design that will be in place for hopefully months or years. Conversely, that tour coming to your town needs a minimal set they can install for sometimes less than a week before heading off to the next city. Shows in New York (or London) are just the best. When I saw *Hadestown* for the first time, it was a national tour, I was sitting high up in a large venue, and I barely remember it. Then when I saw *Hadestown* on Broadway, in its significantly smaller theatre with a superior cast, superior set and sound, superior lighting, and a better seat, my jaw dropped as I then experienced what would become one of my all-time favorite musicals.

The national tour of *Wicked* is one of the highest quality national tours out there, and yet, the Broadway production is somehow still significantly better. With the tour, I usually leave thinking either Glinda or Elphaba was better for that specific night, but on Broadway, they are both excellent. With *Disney's The Lion King*, you get an outstanding production with the tour, but on Broadway, as of this writing, you get Gavin Lee as Scar!

The touring Scar, no matter how good, just isn't going to give you the same experience you will get from Gavin's Scar.

This is probably a good time to share the bad news: you will absolutely need to lower your expectations ahead of attending your next show in your hometown after you experience a show on Broadway or Off-Broadway!

3

WHY DO YOU NEED THIS BOOK?

Chances are, you have seen a play or musical at your local community theatre or at a high school. Maybe it has been a minute since you have seen a show on Broadway, or maybe this will be your first time! Perhaps you live in or near a city where *Broadway Across America* brings national tours of Broadway hits to theatres across the country. Attending these local shows is fairly straightforward, and you typically purchase either a season subscription or individual show tickets. Seeing shows in New York is a bit different, starting with show selection, as there are just so many shows to choose from! Instead of your local theatre telling you, "This is the show you can see right now," you suddenly have forty-one Broadway theatres plus at least as many Off-Broadway theatres to choose from! The prices can be all over the place, and scammers are increasingly aggressive. You are smart to be doing your homework and reading this book before buying expensive theatre tickets.

For the most part, topics in this book are relevant for both Broadway and Off-Broadway shows in New York City, and I will be specific when it matters. I will of course explain the difference between Broadway and Off-Broadway, as many people misunderstand the meanings, but you will have to be patient and wait a bit. I cannot explain everything in this introduction!

This book covers the who, what, when, where, how, and why of going to see a Broadway or Off-Broadway show, including how to pick a show and a seat, what to wear, when to arrive, what not to do, and more. This book is focused on Broadway and Off-Broadway in New York City. If you are seeing multiple shows, the order and time of day can matter. Terminology will be explained, and common mistakes will be discussed. This book will even help you with your intermission restroom strategy (the restroom lines can be very, very long). I also cover accessibility, including sensory accessibility, for neurodivergent theatre lovers.

After reading this book, you will know how to pick a show and a seat like a pro, and you will increase your chances of getting an autograph and picture with one of your favorite stars. You will learn about Broadway, Off-Broadway, and how they differ from your local and regional theatres. This book will even explain the spelling of theatre versus theater. Theatre etiquette is also discussed. While you will observe firsthand many etiquette violations, at least you will be informed and not be the one the cast is talking about backstage.

As of this writing, there are over thirty Broadway shows currently running, and ticket prices are anywhere from $40 to $1500! The ticket prices can vary wildly. Your budget might not allow you to see every show you would like to see, so it is important to prioritize and find the optimal show with the best seat at the best price, and then you want to purchase them through a legitimate source. It is not always obvious which source is the official box office, and even legitimate resellers can tack on additional fees you do not pay when you purchase through the official box office. This book will also explain how to take advantage of "rush tickets" and "lottery tickets," which can offer excellent seats at a steep discount. And I will teach you how you can even get very good seats to a sold-out show.

4

TERMINOLOGY

Instead of overwhelming you with pages and pages of terminology, this section will provide you with just the basic terminology you need to get started, like understanding Broadway versus Off-Broadway and play versus musical. Now play versus musical might sound obvious, but sometimes people incorrectly call a play with music a musical when it is not a musical and is in fact just a play that happens to have some singing. The main difference is that in a musical, the songs actually advance the plot of the story. I will then define additional terminology, as needed, throughout the book.

What exactly is Broadway? What makes up Broadway? Many people wrongly assume Broadway theatres all exist on a street called Broadway, and the venues not on the road Broadway are called Off-Broadway. Nope. In fact, most Broadway theatres are not on the road called Broadway, and a Broadway theatre and an Off-Broadway theatre can actually be physically next door to each other or even in the same building. For example, Lincoln Center Theater has an Off-Broadway theatre in the basement of its Broadway theatre. They share an entrance. It is true that all Broadway theatres are in the same general area, typically defined as the part of Manhattan between 41st and 54th Streets and between 6th and 8th Avenues. This is referred to as the Theatre District, which is located within Times Square in Manhattan, New York City.

The road named Broadway is actually thirty-three miles long, so it wouldn't be very helpful to just have them all be on this long road. Thankfully, they are mostly close to each other. Off-Broadway theatres can be a bit farther away (or not).

The terms Broadway and Off-Broadway actually refer primarily to the capacity of the theatres. A Broadway theatre has a minimum of 500 seats, whereas an Off-Broadway theatre has between 100-499 seats. An Off-Broadway theatre does need to be located within Manhattan to be considered Off-Broadway. A theatre with less than 100 seats and in New York City is referred to as an Off-Off-Broadway theatre. If you hear the term Off-Off-Off-Broadway, this is just a fun term and is not official. The official designations are Off-Off-Broadway (1-99 seats), Off-Broadway (100-499 seats), and Broadway (500 or more seats).

Only shows in Broadway venues are eligible for Tony Award consideration, and Broadway productions typically also come with more union protections for those involved. As a side note, you may hear the terms equity tour and non-equity in the context of national tours. Equity tours follow specific union requirements, and non-equity tours feature non-union performers. Usually, but not always, an equity tour will be of a higher production quality and will have more experienced cast members than a non-equity tour.

A fun website is thebroadwaymap.com, which not only shows you a map of the Broadway theatres but also shows you what is playing where. Of course, be sure to double check your tickets, in case the show has changed venues since the map was last updated. This usually only happens when a show transfers from Off-Broadway to Broadway, or vice versa, but you want to be sure you are going to the right show at the right theatre at the right time on the right day, and your ticket is key here. Please be sure to double check the details on your ticket! Mistakes are surprisingly common.

All Broadway theatres except for the Vivian Beaumont Theatre (at Lincoln Center Theater) are in the same general area (but, as mentioned, most are not on the street named Broadway).

The Museum of Broadway sells a t-shirt that has a map of all the Broadway theatres, and the museum itself has an exhibit that explains the history behind each theatre. The museum is a lot of fun and highly recommended, but it is more enjoyable if you go during an off-peak time. It can be crowded in the summer or during other peak travel periods. The busiest tourist times in New York City are June through August (especially after school is out; I find July to be much more crowded than June), Thanksgiving through New Year's Day, Spring Break (March-April), and long holiday weekends. It is probably actually simpler to state when New York is less crowded: January, February, mid-September, October, and early November. The first week in December can also be nice. Many of the holiday decorations are up, and the tourism slows down a bit between the Thanksgiving crowd and the Christmas crowd.

While you might assume Off-Broadway is inferior to Broadway, the intimate experience of a theatre with less than 500 seats can be very enjoyable. And you can absolutely see the biggest star names Off-Broadway, and you can sometimes have an easier time meeting them after the show at a smaller venue. For example, Hugh Jackman and Tom Hanks both performed in Off-Broadway productions in 2025.

A key motivation for transferring to Broadway is to be eligible for the Tony Awards. Also, if a hit show can fill the venue, it can potentially make more money in a larger Broadway venue (it can also lose more money more quickly if it is a flop). Therefore, your best hit shows will indeed often be on Broadway. Broadway is also more convenient location-wise, assuming you are spending your time midtown near Times Square, since some Off-Broadway venues might be a couple of miles away downtown, for example.

Even the larger Broadway venues can be significantly smaller than regional theatres throughout the United States where tour productions play, so an experience on Broadway can be significantly more intimate than the same show's national tour at your local theatre. From a patron perspective, bigger is not necessarily better, and having your favorite star a few feet away from you at a Broadway or Off-Broadway production can be very exciting.

Next on the terminology list, when looking at a cast list, you may see the terms principal, ensemble, standby, understudy, and swing. A principal role is any role that is considered to be a lead role or a featured role. These roles are typically considered to be important to advancing the plot. The other roles are considered part of the ensemble.

Both a standby and an understudy cover for a principal role when the main performer is unavailable, which might be known ahead of time or can be a surprise, for example if a performer becomes sick or injured. It can also happen in the middle of a show! More on that in a moment.

The key difference between a standby and an understudy is that the standby is not otherwise in the show and is effectively "on call" to step in at any moment. Conversely, an understudy performs in the ensemble except when needed to cover a lead or supporting role.

When an understudy needs to fill in, then someone needs to cover the understudy's normal role in the ensemble. This is where a swing comes in. A swing covers an understudy who is either covering for another role or out sick. If a swing then gets injured or sick, a different swing covers for that swing.

What is amazing about standbys, understudies, and swings is they are often prepared to cover multiple roles, and they might even have to change mid-show! Think about this. They have to learn the lines, the songs, the stage movement and blocking, and the characters of multiple roles! In the case of a significant lead character, the standby might only cover that one character. But understudies and swings are almost always covering more than one character. So when that standby, understudy, or swing goes on stage, please cheer extra loudly! They worked very hard to get this moment!

You might assume that the standby or understudy or swing is an inferior performer to the lead, but it might just be the opinion of those who did the casting. And sometimes, once the big star's contract is up, that actor's standby or understudy might then take over the role full-time. I have seen shows where I enjoyed the standby or understudy's performance more than I did the performance of the usual lead. This is the understudy's moment to shine, so the hungry understudy might actually put more effort, energy, and presence into the performance than would a lead who is feeling ill and just struggling to get through the show. It can be especially exciting and emotional if you are seeing the understudy's Broadway debut or even just the actor's debut in the role.

I mentioned this "on call" can happen in the middle of a show. Dancers can get injured, and swings are jumping in to cover ensemble members throughout the show without you even noticing. An announcement is typically only made if it is a named character being replaced. And this can happen at any point in the show.

For example, at one performance of the national tour of *Dear Evan Hansen*, the actor playing Evan Hansen was missing his notes in the beginning of Act I. This is not normal and is not a skills issue; Broadway performers do not miss their notes. It seemed apparent the actor was experiencing some form of vocal injury. So, at the end of one of the scenes, we got an announcement over the intercom: "We are holding, actors please clear the stage." This is referred to as a "stage hold" and is rare in a professional production.

We then had a forty-minute delay, followed by an announcement, "for the rest of tonight's performance, the character Evan Hansen will be played by..." followed by unusual loud cheers from backstage. The forty-minute delay was to call this actor into the theatre, get the actor into costume and make-up, and to warm up vocally. When the replacement actor came on, he appeared a bit nervous at first and then did an absolutely outstanding job. He then cried during the bows at the end of the show, which then made all of us in the audience cry. It was apparently his stage debut, partway during the show so not even getting to start from the beginning. It was one of the most special live theatre moments I have experienced. As they say, the show must go on!

Now sometimes, they do unfortunately run out of cast members, for example if a virus is running through the entire cast, and then they do have to sometimes cancel a performance. But usually they can find someone. In July 2025, *Moulin Rouge* on Broadway had run out of healthy actors for the role Satine, and the show finally found Nicci Claspell, who had never before performed on Broadway but had performed the role Satine in the national tour production more than a year earlier. With no rehearsals and only two hours notice, Nicci successfully tapped into her muscle memory and allowed the show to go on—with no rehearsal![1] How exciting for the audience and for the cast that night. And how exciting for Nicci to make her Broadway debut with just two hours notice!

Continuing on with some terminology, first there are

---

1. Source: https://www.broadwayworld.com/article/Nicci-Claspell-Steps-Into-MOULIN-ROUGE-With-Two-Hours-Notice-No-Rehearsal-20250710

rehearsals, then preview performances, and then Opening Night. When purchasing tickets, discussed later in the book, you might find it confusing that Opening Night actually takes place after what looks like the show's opening. Before Opening Night, there are preview performances. Some patrons mistakenly call the first preview show the "opening night," but it is actually called "First Preview" (which is also exciting but for different reasons).

First Preview is special enough that audience members frequently get a free gift for attending, and the audience is often filled with the producers and family and friends of the cast. So, if you are debating between First Preview and the second preview, pick First Preview if you can! Just know that it might be rough, and things could go wrong. This is part of the fun! Just be careful to not criticize a performer you don't like, because you might be sitting next to that performer's mom! Don't be the person who kills her joy and proud moment. I can't tell you how often I find myself sitting next to someone who is the parent, partner, or good friend of a cast member. It's a small world. Do talk to the people around you, as everyone has fun stories and interesting backgrounds.

Preview performances allow the director to further fine-tune the show based on audience reactions. Preview performances can be rough, and the show might actually stop, for example if a prop or part of the set is not working properly. Preview performances can be very exciting, as you are seeing the magic being fine-tuned. You might see actors forget their lines and have to improvise, and you might see other actors covering their lines and helping their scene partners get through it. But chances are, you will not even realize this is happening unless you know the script.

Each night after a preview performance, the production may get further modified. Jokes that don't land might get deleted. The script will be fine-tuned perhaps to make scenes tighter, by deleting lines. The show does not get locked in until Opening Night, which is sometimes also referred to as Press Night. Opening Night is frequently invitation-only, and it is the premiere where the theatre critics and other stars come to see the unveiling of the show.

The show is now locked in, and the director has now handed off the show. Even though the show is now finalized, actors might continue fine-tuning nuances in their performances as they get to know their characters even better. Especially in locally produced theatre outside of New York, the quality of a show can continue improving as it goes on. The Closing Night performance might be fairly different from the Opening Night performance, because by then the actors know their characters so well.

Conversely, on Broadway, the shows tend to be high quality even by dress rehearsals and previews, as the actors were likely developing their characters in depth even before the first rehearsal. Also, many shows do out of town "tryouts" before transferring to Broadway, to make sure they are in good shape even before that First Preview in New York.

In general, there is no real reason to avoid seeing a preview performance on Broadway, even though it may get improved in the weeks ahead. You will be one of the first to see the show, and your ticket price might be lower than if you wait until later. Just have a positive attitude knowing the show is still getting fine-tuned. The more experienced the cast, the less likely there are to be actual differences in the preview performances. If you have friends in the industry, you might be lucky enough to get invited to a dress rehearsal prior to First Preview. This is sometimes referred to as "Invited Dress." It is meant to be a safe, supportive audience for the actors as they deliver their lines in front of an audience for the first time. Definitely attend a rehearsal if you get an invitation, but then also remember to cheer loudly.

Lastly, let's discuss the spelling. Is it theatre or theater? I am going to explain both (1) why technically, either is correct, but (2) there actually is a difference. Of course, technically, "theatre" is just the British spelling, and "theater" is the American spelling. But for theatre fans, there is more to it. Many people use the *theatre* spelling to refer to the art itself, while the *theater* spelling is used to describe a physical venue. For me, I tend to use theater when I am describing a movie theater, a performing arts venue that has chosen to use the "theater" spelling, or when I am clearly just talking about a building. In all other references to live theatre, I tend to use the theatre spelling.

As an example, I might refer to someone performing theatre at the theater. But I also might say theatre at the theatre to emphasize the organization's enablement of art more so than the physical structure. But again, either is technically correct.

5

ACCESSIBILITY

If you have accessibility needs, be sure to research the accommodations at each venue, as this may limit your show options. Some venues, especially historical theatres, might not have elevators or other accommodations. Accessibility is downright horrible at some venues. Their historical landmark nature makes them exempt from accessibility requirements, and it might also just simply be impossible or impractical to modify the historical building.

Some productions designate specific performances to have ASL interpreters, live captioning, sensory-friendly or autism-friendly productions, relaxed audiences, and other accommodations. In New York, the website tdf.org lists specific autism-friendly performances where the production is modified and the audience etiquette is relaxed, so neurodivergent patrons can enjoy live theatre from the main auditorium without judgment from other patrons. In my experience, neurodivergent audience members at sensory-friendly performances practice far better theatre etiquette than adults who have had one or more too many alcoholic beverages before a show.

From a show's official website, you can look for the Accessibility menu option to learn more about the specific offerings at that venue. Many theatres have a phone number dedicated to accessibility questions, and some venues have a separate entrance that may be more accessible for some physical disabilities.

Remember that many disabilities are invisible, so it is never appropriate to judge or comment on another patron's unusual behavior or usage of accessibility accommodations. At the tour of the improv show, *Whose Live Anyway,* an audience participation patron was struggling to walk up on the stage. At first glance, she appeared intoxicated and therefore unable to walk up the steps. She ended up actually crawling up the steps to the stage in what again appeared to be intoxication. The talent at the show apparently had proper training, and they remained quiet instead of making comments or jokes about her seeming to have had too much to drink. We then learned she was physically disabled, completely sober, and was struggling to walk up on stage due to the lack of a handrail. How fortunate the comedians had proper training to not jump to making jokes, as they would have been making jokes about her disability. Another example is if you see a patron wearing large headphones, this is likely a sensory accommodation to lower the noise level. No patron wants attention called to a disability or to an accommodation.

6

PICKING A SHOW

Picking a show is harder than you might at first expect. There are so many good shows! While you might be inclined to just default to *Hamilton* or *Wicked*, which are both excellent shows, let me tell you why you should also consider newer shows with their original casts.

My rule of thumb is to first prioritize hit shows that may be closing soon, shows that still have their original casts, and shows that have that big star you have always wanted to see. If there is a show that checks all three of these boxes, that's a great one to prioritize! *Hamilton* and *Wicked* will likely still be there during your next trip to New York, but that new show with your favorite star might close soon. If not, your star might be replaced, as the big stars only stay in the cast for so long.

Additionally, both *Hamilton* and *Wicked* have very good national tours that you could see at home, freeing up a precious New York slot for a new work. Once a new show closes, you might never be able to see it ever again. This is especially true if the show did not win any Tony Awards, as many national tours end up being just the Tony Award winning shows. That said, in my opinion, both *Hamilton* and *Wicked* in New York are indeed even higher quality than their tours, so it is not a wrong choice to choose one of these outstanding shows for a precious show slot.

You could start by visiting previewnight.com and looking at the "Must See" or Critic's Pick shows. These are the best of the best shows that are still currently open. Or visit broadwayholi dayguide.com or broadwayguidenyc.com to see if a recent guide is published. Then see if any of these shows are closing soon but still open during your trip. Also look to see if there are any big stars you would love to see on stage. The sites playbil l.com and broadway.com can be good resources for researching the shows. Playbill has great news and articles, while Broad-way.com will let you filter by date to see what shows are actu-ally playing during your trip.

Know that most shows run Tuesday-Sunday with matinees typically only on Wednesday, Saturday, and Sunday. This works out to eight performances over six days. Some shows, especially newer shows or Off-Broadway shows, may offer Monday shows or matinees on non-standard days where they have less compe-tition. If there is a show you want to see that offers a Monday performance or a matinee on a non-standard day, and if you are wanting to see multiple shows during your trip, then absolutely book this show for that Monday or non-standard matinee slot instead of tying up one of the other precious evening slots, as this will then let you get more shows in. When you are purchasing your ticket, take your time to make sure you notice any alerts, such as "[Big Star Name] will not be performing at this performance" or "...will not be performing the weeks of...."

Lastly, take a look at the prices on different days, as the cost can vary quite a bit from day to day, depending on the supply and demand for tickets for a given show day. Many shows use dynamic pricing, meaning the prices go up as there are fewer seats left. This means for popular shows, you frequently want to purchase your tickets in advance. They can be sold out if you wait too long. For shows you are okay missing if sold out, there are also strategies for last minute deeply discounted tickets, which will be discussed later.

Next, let's discuss Broadway vs. Off-Broadway a bit more. As previously explained, this refers primarily to the theatre's capacity. The big hits are more often going to be in a Broadway theatre, while the newer shows or long-running shows may be at an Off-Broadway venue, perhaps to keep the show's costs down. Fun long-running shows to see Off-Broadway include *Little Shop of Horrors* and *The Play That Goes Wrong*. Some of my all-time favorite shows have been performed Off-Broadway and have not (yet?) transferred to Broadway.

If you are scheduling two (or more?!) shows in one day, note the run time of the matinee, to make sure you leave yourself enough time to grab dinner before your evening show. Also be careful about choosing a heavy or emotional show as your matinee, as you may need time to process what you just experienced. If you immediately jump into your evening show, you are cheating yourself out of the experience of fully processing the incredible art you experienced at the matinee. A short ninety-minute comedy can be a good choice for a matinee if you are also seeing an evening show. Or if you see a heavy matinee, try to have a lighter show that night. That said, these are just optimization tips, so do whatever gets you the best seat at the best price. The trick to doing a three-show day, if so inclined, is to find a ninety-minute matinee that offers a 5 PM start time, and make sure your first matinee will finish in time. Shows like *Oh, Mary!* and *Beau the Musical* sometimes schedule 5 PM start times to let you squeeze them in between two other shows. But this can be stressful, and a maximum of one show per day is optimal.

Only we true theatre nerds do two-show and three-show days (I have heard of someone doing a five-show day). I have only done a three-show day once (*Gruesome Playground Injuries,*

Beau the Musical, Just In Time), and I am not sure I will do it again. Even with two-show days, I sometimes feel like I cheat myself out of fully processing the matinee before jumping in to the next show. If you are from the west coast and debating between a matinee and an evening show, know that matinee time can be hard if it is the first or second day after your travel day.

When picking your show(s), in the end, know there is really no wrong choice. Well, actually the wrong choice would be to see zero shows. Chances are, you will enjoy whatever you see, and you will not be able to see every show you want to see. Despite what I wrote earlier about what types of shows to prioritize seeing, if you just really want to see *Hamilton*, *Wicked*, or *Disney's The Lion King* on Broadway, then do it! As good as the national tours are, these shows are indeed even better on Broadway. Just be sure to consider other shows like *Hadestown*, *Ragtime*, *Mexodus*, *Every Brilliant Thing*, and the latest Tony Award "Best Musical" or "Best Play."

If you are seeing multiple shows, it can be fun to have a mix of plays and musicals and a mix of Broadway and Off-Broadway, as they can be very different experiences. You might be assuming you will enjoy a big musical on Broadway the most (and you will enjoy it!), but then a play you have never heard of in a tiny 100 seat Off-Broadway venue is the one you can't stop talking about for months after your trip. This happens to me all the time.

7

PICKING YOUR SEAT
AND BUYING A TICKET

B uckle up, as this is by far the longest chapter in this
book. There is much to cover to make sure you get the
best seat for the best price.

The safest way to buy your ticket is from the show's official
site. When you do an Internet search for your show, I suggest
ignoring all of the "Sponsored" results at the top of the search
results page, and start reading the search results below all of
the "Sponsored" links. Even if one of the sponsored results
seems like the official site, clicking that sponsored link will
cause the theatre to have to then pay the search engine
company money for your click. Clicking the "organic" non-
sponsored link slightly lower on the page does not cost the
theatre money. The search engine company has plenty of
money and generally much more money than do the theatres,
so why transfer more money from the theatres to the wealthy
tech company? This behavior tweak helps the theatre while
also making sure you do not click on any potentially deceptive
"sponsored" results, which can include high price ticket
scalpers.

By purchasing your tickets directly from the show's official online box office, you are avoiding extra fees that may be charged by third party ticket sellers, for example some of the ones that may be in those "Sponsored" search results (they need your extra fee to pay the tech company for that premium placement). You can sometimes avoid even more fees by calling up the box office and purchasing your tickets over the phone, or in-person at the box office window, but you may find the convenience of purchasing from the show's online box office is worth any online fees, since you also get to pick out your seat from a visual seating chart.

PICKING YOUR SEAT

I will first explain some terminology and then share both the popular thinking as well as my own preferences as to which are the best seats, if budget is not your primary concern. I will then discuss more budget-friendly options. This is a topic where it's going to be different if you are by yourself or with others or with kids.

The "Orchestra" section is the floor seating on the main level of the theatre. It includes the seats closest to the stage and near the orchestra pit as well as the seats way in the back. Always make sure you first orient the seating chart to where the stage is located, so you don't accidentally book the last row thinking you are getting front row. Many show websites will include a visual seating chart. Orchestra seats near the stage and in the center are considered premium, while orchestra seats near the back can sometimes make it harder to see. Front row orchestra is controversial and varies by venue (discussed more in a bit). Also, Row A is not necessarily front row! This will also be explained.

The upper levels have various names including loge, mezzanine, and balcony. Typically, loge is better than mezzanine, which is better than balcony. But some venues might just have balcony seating, or they might have multiple levels of balcony. In general, the higher up and farther away you are, the harder it will be to see.

If you are attending with children, then front row of the lowest "balcony" (might be called loge or mezzanine) is frequently going to be your best bet, as nobody will be in front of you blocking their view. The upper level also typically has a better slope than does the orchestra section, so in general, the kids will have an easier time seeing from this upper level even if not in front row, as long as you are close to the front row.

Many venues do offer booster seats, but these are only a good idea if your kids are able to sit still and won't be moving around and playing with the booster seat throughout the show, as this will annoy you and everyone around you. If you can get in the first two or three rows (ideally front row) of the lowest level of the upper level, this is likely the best. However, *Wicked* at the Gershwin Theatre is one venue where I feel like the balcony is far away, but yet it still might be better than your regional tour theatre back home. Therefore, with *Wicked*, I would try to get closer in the Orchestra section, if possible, and deal with a booster seat, due to the balcony being farther back. That said, this is just a preference, and you can still have an amazing time from the balcony.

If you are attending a show by yourself, and if the venue has two aisles in the Orchestra section as many do (e.g., Orchestra Left, aisle, Orchestra Center, aisle, Orchestra Right), then an inside aisle seat in either Orchestra Left or Orchestra Right can offer you an unobstructed diagonal view to the stage if you are say five to eight rows back from the stage. I don't like to be any closer or farther away than this when doing this trick on the side. I don't like this when you have a guest, as then your guest is a bit too far to the side without any viewing advantage.

If you are with adult guests, the popular view is center orchestra perhaps four to ten rows back is the best. These are often where the "house seats" are located. House seats are a handful of seats the "house" (the venue) holds back for VIPs, famous guests, guests of the cast, critics, major donors, the show's producers or investors, or anyone who might request a seat at the last minute and is expecting a good seat. For example, a show's producers would want an investor or a critic to have a good seat and the best possible experience. These house seats usually get released anywhere from twenty-four hours to one to two weeks prior to the performance date, so if you do not love your seat, check in with the box office to see if you can get a better seat (but you might have to pay the difference in price).

I mentioned front row orchestra is controversial ("too close!" many say), but personally this is often my favorite place to sit, especially if the show features a star. There are indeed tradeoffs. You will be looking up, you might not be able to see the performers' feet, and you cannot take in the whole show the way you could from front row balcony. But in the front row, I have had both Bernadette Peters and Patti LuPone look me directly in the eye as they sang right to me. I have had Hugh Jackman sit down on the edge of the stage in front of me and make direct eye contact while speaking to me, I have had Roxie in *Chicago* toss me a (plastic) red rose, and I have been asked to play a cowbell with the cast during the final scene of a show (it is surprisingly high stress and pressure to keep the beat for several minutes in front of hundreds of patrons—but oh so fun).

At the national tour of *Les Misérables,* I decided to test out the pros and cons of various seating options, and I saw two performances in one day (and four performances that week). At the matinee, I sat in front row center mezzanine, and at the evening show, I sat in front row orchestra. At this particular venue, front row orchestra was sadly still fairly far away from the cast, whereas in New York, the cast can be just feet away.

But even at this farther distance, I could hear ensemble chatter that I could not hear up in the balcony, as this chatter was not picked up by the microphones. This added a new dimension that was fun. But due to a very high stage, I could not see the performers' feet. Up in the mezzanine, I had a much better view of the set and of the choreography. All that said, I booked a seat as close as I could get for *Les Misérables* at Radio City Music Hall in July 2026. This may turn out to be a mistake, because this production will also incorporate large screens, and I will not be able to as easily take in the full staging and choreography. But I just like to be close and with nobody in front of me. Follow @brianguytheatre and @preview_night on Instagram to see what I have to say about my choice at that show!

Many New York stages are low enough that front row ends up being an incredible experience. At touring venues, it can be a bit more dangerous to do front row, as the stages can be higher up, making it harder to see. I have never once had a bad experience in front row orchestra at a show in New York.

One caution is you will get spit on, as many professional Broadway singers spray saliva all over the place as they are singing. It's not just Jonathan Groff. Numerous performers have spit on me (immersive!), Jonathan Groff's scene partners in *Just In Time* flung sweat all over me as they tossed their hair, and I had to briefly close my eyes once when one Broadway star was spraying just so much (remember, you are often looking up when in front row). It is a literal splash zone, but we true Broadway fans agree you want to sit where you can get spit on.

If this is not your thing, go at least two or three rows back. At *Sondheim's Old Friends*, even the patrons behind me in second row said they got spit on, due to just how close the stage was to the front rows, and due to how far downstage the performers came (it was an incredible experience).

It is worth mentioning there is also a small risk in front row that props can unexpectedly hit you, especially during early

Preview performances. This is not common nor intentional, but I have had it happen a few times (I see a lot of shows), almost always during a Preview performance. I forget what show it was where glass was shattered during a dramatic scene, and the glass flew off the stage and went all over my lap. It of course startled me, and the cast was horrified (it was a mistake). But it was some kind of stage glass, called "stunt glass," that is safe, designed for theatre, and it did not nor could not cut me. They apologized after the show, but I thought it was immersive and fantastic! That's one reason I love to sit in the front row. After all, it was having "rain" kicked all over me during a performance of "Singin' in the Rain" that got me hooked on theatre in the first place. In *Little Shop of Horrors*, front row is intentionally an immersive "splash zone" and is oh so fun.

For me, not being tall, I prioritize being able to see, so I almost always do front row orchestra, front row loge, or inside aisle on a side orchestra section. The few times I have done premium orchestra center seats several rows back (what are considered the best seats in the house), I have so far almost always ended up being lucky with a short person in front of me, but I have also had experiences where I am leaning and struggling to see the whole show. If I need to select a row in center orchestra, I always try to find out where the slope starts, as sometimes there is zero slope within the first several rows of orchestra. The site aViewFromMySeat.com can be helpful, and some ticketing sites also show a preview of the view. Try to move the view angle if you can to see where the step up exists. For example, the first three rows might be at the same level, and then the next several rows might be a step up. In that scenario, I would grab the fourth row, the first row that is up the slope a bit.

Every venue is different. Sometimes it pays to just call up the Box Office and ask their opinions, as they are usually knowledgeable and will tell you their favorite places to sit. At some venues, the loge, mezzanine, or balcony can feel too far away, while at other venues, it is fairly close. The seating chart will tell you how close the overhang is. For example, the mezzanine overhang at *Wicked* at the Gershwin Theatre comes out at Row N, which is actually the seventeenth row, since Row A in Orchestra is actually the fifth row. The first row is actually Row BB, and rows two to four are actually rows CC-EE. See why it is important to look at the seating chart? It is always sad to see someone so excited to be sitting in the front row, because they have Row A, only to be eventually asked by an usher to move back several rows to their Row A seat. This happens a lot!

The venue is not trying to be deceptive; they just have some shows that will not have the closer rows BB-EE, and as you can see, they do not have a row AA at *Wicked*. It is not practical for them to renumber the seats with each show, so this numbering scheme gives them flexibility to add or remove rows of seats in the front, depending on the stage configuration and whether or not there is an orchestra. Other shows in the future at Gershwin Theatre might have a row AA inserted, or they might have all rows removed up to Row A, indeed making Row A the first row.

At *Wicked*, you might feel like front row mezzanine is actually too far away, whereas conversely, when *Cabaret at the Kit Kat Club* was playing at the August Wilson Theatre, the front row of mezzanine came out at Row D, which is significantly closer. As you can see, it is critical to check the seating chart.

I have a few more comments about front row orchestra, which again varies greatly by venue and by show. If the stage is low enough, I argue there is no greater experience than front row orchestra. Many will strongly disagree with me. But is there such a thing as being "too close" to your favorite stars? My absolute favorite theatre experiences have been when I was "too close" in front row orchestra.

The criticisms are true: sometimes you cannot see the stage

floor, the actors' feet, or other things happening low to the ground. But thanks to these horrible and "too close" front row seats, I have had so many stars look me directly in the eye as they sing directly to me (they can actually see front row, as the lights frequently hit this row). I have been spit on by more stars than I can name as they sing just a few feet away from me. And after the show at the stage door, they remember me and thank me for cheering for them. If you are going to see your favorite star, I say go front row orchestra if you can, even though it is not an optimal view of the show and of the choreography.

If you don't care about anyone in particular in the cast, then the loge can be a great choice, and you will have a great view of everything. A popular consensus is that for plays, it is nice to be closer, and for musicals, it can be nice to be a bit farther back, in order to enjoy all of the choreography. Note that the front one or two rows are sometimes not released until two weeks before the show, so if they are not available when you buy your tickets, check back again two weeks prior to your show. If they suddenly become available, you can call up the box office to get your seat moved; you will just have to pay any difference in price if the seats are now more expensive. You will not get a refund if the tickets are now less expensive.

If you are on the larger size, know that at some venues, the leg room can get quite a bit smaller as you get higher up and into the less expensive seats. As a volunteer usher, I have in the past needed to reseat larger patrons who were not physically able to enter the smaller rows up in the second or third balcony. I was shocked the first time I learned there is sometimes more leg room down in the orchestra rows. However, front row orchestra and front row upper level can sometimes have significantly less leg room.

In general, the box office employees can be very helpful with these types of questions. You can call up, let the employee know you are on the larger size or of a shorter height, etc., and they can educate you about the optimal seats at that venue. Chances are, you are not the first person who has had these questions, and it is much better to address it now than at the show. In my experience, Broadway box office employees are customer service focused and will be non-judgmental in whatever you ask them.

Another consideration is whether or not you have a fear of heights. The front row of the upper level can be an issue for some patrons. It can be high up, and the railing is low. If you are unsure, do not sit here, and instead, walk to this section during intermission to see how you feel, so you will know for next time. These are generally expensive seats, so you do not want to be needing to relocate to cheaper seats—whatever is left—if you find you are not comfortable with the height once you get there. While these heights are nothing like at an arena or a stadium, I have heard enough people say they have issues with front row balcony (and even front row loge) that it is worth raising here.

All that said, some venues have higher balconies than others, so you might be fine at some venues while struggling at other venues. Again, if you are unsure, it is probably just best to avoid front row of the balcony. There is generally enough slope in the upper level that you could likely do second row and possibly eliminate the issue, but again, if unsure, don't risk it and instead check it out during intermission or before or after the show.

THE CHEAP SEATS

What if the least expensive seats, which might still be pretty expensive, are all you can afford? Live theatre is expensive, especially if you are trying to take your family and need multiple seats. Know you will have a good time, no matter where you sit! And remember, Broadway theatres—and especially Off-Broadway theatres—are smaller and more intimate than your big theatre back home, so even the "worst" seats at a Broadway or Off-Broadway house can still be excellent seats. The saying, "there's no bad seat in the house" applies to many shows!

First, when buying tickets, again make sure you are on the show's official box office site and not at a ticket broker's site. If you are at Telecharge or ATG, you are likely at the official box office. When in doubt, go back to the show's official site (not clicking on the top Sponsored Results at the top of your Internet search results), and click Buy Tickets from the show's page.

Second, check other show dates and show times, as prices can vary on different dates. Then check and compare with discount sites such as TKTS and TodayTix.

Also check the Theatr app on your smartphone, to see if current ticketholders are selling their tickets (the Theatr app prohibits them from selling for more than they paid). But do realize the official box office might currently be less expensive than what the Theatr app ticket holder previously paid.

Next, look for discount codes on the show's social media pages. Some shows offer two-for-one or deeply discounted tickets. If this is a hot show with a big star, the prices might just be very high.

At many Broadway and especially Off-Broadway venues, there really isn't a bad seat, due to the smaller theatre sizes. If you are in the absolute back row in the corner of the theatre behind a very tall person, and you can barely see, you will at least still experience the energy from the audience, the joy of the live music, and you were still there. It is better than not going, especially if the ticket is reasonably priced. You can always check in at the box office the day of the show to see if they can help you out with a better seat.

I have heard stories of people with horrible seats getting

moved up to premium seats. They would rather have a good seat full, and they want you to enjoy the show. As for whether you should prioritize being closer but to the side or centered but farther back (in the case of a show that is already full), it really depends on the specific show, and there are of course pros and cons. I have sat close and to the side, and I have sat centered and in the very last row, and I had a great time in both experiences. Given the choice, I would probably choose to be closer and to the side rather than centered and farther back, but it also depends how far to the side? In general, I feel like closer is better.

When I am a volunteer usher, sometimes we sit in the far back of the theatre in the very last row. It is still fun, and I was actually surprised that these "bad seats" are as good as they are!

The hardest decision might be if you are deciding whether to go see your first choice show with a bad seat or your second or third choice show with a great seat. If the first choice is a big star you absolutely want to experience, then that might be the best choice. Otherwise, going to the show with the better seat might be more enjoyable. In this case, I think listen to your gut, but also know there really is not a right or wrong decision. Either show will be fun!

WHEN TO BUY

Another question is how far in advance to buy your tickets. What if you get sick? What if you have to cancel your trip? Very few shows seem to offer cancellation insurance, and for those that do, some insurance policies won't let you do claims for more than one show within so many days (if the same insurance provider).

For a newer show that just won Tony Awards, you are going to want to purchase in advance, as these shows sell out. Examples in 2025 include *Just In Time, Oh, Mary!* and *Maybe Happy*

Ending. For older shows, like *Wicked* or *Hamilton*, you can likely purchase later, unless there is a big name in the show or unless it is a peak tourism period. However, *Hamilton* and *Wicked* are often the number one and number two shows for revenue, and they are usually at capacity, so don't wait too long.

Also, for newer shows, the prices will go up as the word-of-mouth spreads about the show. You might end up doing a mix of purchasing in advance the most important show you absolutely want to see and where you want a good seat, and then you might purchase the older show tickets once you are in town or at least at the airport, knowing you will for sure be there.

I used to buy show tickets in-flight on the airplane, but now I tend to buy most of my tickets well in advance with a few last-minute purchases sometimes even fifteen minutes before curtain time. For last minute purchases, you can see if rush or lottery tickets are an option, as explained next. You might not know how tired you are until the day of, so one strategy if you want to see many shows is book up your evening slots but keep your matinee slots open. Then on Wednesday morning, you can make a spontaneous choice whether or not you will add a matinee that day (remember most shows only have matinees on Wednesdays, Saturdays, and Sundays). Or enter the lottery the day before (or week before, depending on the show) and see if you win cheap tickets.

RUSH AND LOTTERY TICKETS

The theatre wants the venue to be full, so they unload any unsold seats at steep discounts at the last minute. Sometimes these are the best house seats they were holding for any last-minute VIPs.

Many shows offer a digital lottery where you enter the day before or the week before. A typical price might be $49 for a seat that might otherwise be many hundreds of dollars. Each show works a bit differently, so you need to go to the show's official website and look for the details about the lottery. You are usually not on the hook if you win, so you can enter multiple lotteries, see which ones you win (if any), and then decide which show to book. In the case of *Hamilton*, you enter the lottery from the show's mobile app the week before. If you are visiting during a peak tourism month, your show might be truly sold out, but some shows like *Hamilton* always allocate some lottery tickets (they do this to provide financial accessibility).

The TKTS ticket booth is a popular option that offers same-day tickets and sometimes next-day matinee tickets for up to fifty percent off. The catch is that you do not know what your seat will be until after you purchase your tickets. There is a TKTS mobile app and the tdf.org website where you can learn more about current offerings. Remember to only transact at the actual ticket booth, as anyone approaching you while you are in line may be trying to scam you.

The Theatr mobile app is a marketplace where patrons list their tickets for sale when they can no longer attend. The seller will generally text you, e-mail you, or hand deliver the tickets, so you do need to be comfortable exchanging contact info and/or meeting in person.

Rush tickets are typically same-day tickets you can often get for $25-$60 instead of several hundreds of dollars. You might not be able to get seats together. Not every show offers rush tickets, so you need to check the show's official website. Digital lottery and TKTS seem to be more common in New York.

If you plan to purchase your tickets at retail price from the website, it's a good idea to first check the show's official social media accounts, for example Instagram and Facebook, to see if they are offering any discount codes. Then just remember to actually plug in the discount code before you check out!

SOLD OUT SHOWS

There are a couple of tricks when that show you really want to see is sold out. First, check the Theatr app, as previously mentioned, as you might find good seats at a great price (sellers cannot charge more than they paid and will often discount them in order to sell them). Second, if the venue is a non-profit theatre, such as Lincoln Center Theater, MCC, or the Public Theatre, and if your budget is higher, it may be possible for you to get house seats as a donor benefit if you make a donation of a certain dollar value.

House seats are sometimes held back for donors or other VIP needs. If donating fits your budget, it can be a way to get access to these great seats. Check out the venue's donor page for details. With some shows, for example *Ragtime* at Lincoln Center Theater, a donation that includes two complimentary house seats as a donor benefit might not be much more expensive than the price of premium tickets outright, and good seats might not otherwise be available. And the donor benefit might give you access to purchase house seats for every future show that season at Lincoln Center Theater.

Similarly, a donation to MCC might get you complimentary house seats to their shows. The key is to arrange for this at least a few weeks in advance, since the house seats might be sold out, or they might be released to the public if you wait too long.

Note that policies vary by organization, and donor benefits often change from season to season.

Always check out the donor benefits to see what the perks are, as this can help you with sold out shows while you support a great cause at the same time.

PERFORMER ALERTS

If you are wanting to track whether or not your performance will feature a standby, understudy, or swing, check out the website understudies.org. Just note that sometimes these replacements are made at the last minute (or even during the show), but the site can help you with planned absences or unexpected absences recently announced. Also check your e-mail the day of your show to see if the venue is letting you know your star is out. You need to request any refund before the show starts, if you are entitled to a refund (more on this in a bit).

SHOW RESEARCH

It can be fun to do research about your upcoming show, but be careful of spoilers! It can be so much more fun to be surprised during a show, for example during a very funny scene.

Some shows have behind the scenes vlogs on YouTube. These can be fun to watch. Check out the Broadway.com channel on YouTube to search for these vlogs, or search YouTube for the title of your show. But again, be careful, as some video reviews will give you spoilers without warning you first. The site previewnight.com will generally work hard to avoid any spoilers in its reviews.

Original cast recordings are also a fun way to learn the music of a show ahead of time. Tip: these are called cast recordings, not soundtracks. A cast recording includes the music and occasionally some dialog from the musical. These songs are sung by the cast members and advance the plot and story. Conversely, a soundtrack is from a film or TV show and includes songs that are present in the show, but these songs in a soundtrack do not necessarily advance the story. Do know that cast recordings can occasionally include spoilers, but the producers are generally careful to avoid this.

If your musical is also a movie, be careful when searching Spotify, Apple Music, Tidal, or your favorite music streaming service to search for the original cast recording and not for the soundtrack. Also, if your musical is a revival, take note of the year. For example, *Les Misérables* has a soundtrack from the 2012 movie, an Original Cast Recording from the 1985 production in London, an Original Cast Recording from the 1987 production on Broadway, multiple Staged Concert versions, and more! You can preview tracks from each to determine which you like best. But for some shows, the cast recording may have a different song selection than what is on the soundtrack for a movie. For example, *Moulin Rouge* the 2019 musical has different songs compared to *Moulin Rouge* the movie. And for shows like *& Juliet* that started in London, the Original London Cast Recording has different stars singing compared to the Original Broadway Cast Recording. It is important to pay attention to the details, to make sure you get what you expect (this is of course more important when ordering vinyl than it is when listening on streaming).

REFUNDS AND EXCHANGES

Generally, there are no refunds or exchanges. However, it never hurts to call the box office, explain your situation, and see if they will help. I have had shows give me refunds, and I have had shows say no. They will often offer a date exchange, but the new date might now be more expensive for worse seats. However, if a performer who is featured "above the title" is unexpectedly absent, you are generally entitled to a refund, as long as you purchased your tickets from the official box office and request the refund before the show starts. If you purchased elsewhere, then you would need to check that seller's refund policies. It's a good idea to check your e-mail before the show for any absence announcement. You can also check the under studies.org website, although it may not have any last-minute callouts.

If the box office line is huge for the refund, you can sometimes just reply to the e-mail alert letting you know the star is out, if they give you this option in the e-mail (assuming you purchased your tickets directly from the official box office and assuming the box office sends out this notice). Be careful not to reply to a no-reply e-mail address and instead address your refund request to the e-mail address they tell you to use (e.g., ticketing@...). You should then likely get a refund within a few days, as long as your reply is timestamped before the start of the show.

In my experience, they do not reply to your e-mail (due to the volume), but you will indeed see a refund usually within a few days. If this is all happening at the last minute and you would not be able to see a different show instead, I encourage you to stick with the show and go support the replacement, who might be incredible. I have from time to time enjoyed the understudy's performance even more.

Regarding exchanges, if you later change your mind and prefer a different seat or a different show date or time, just call up the box office. Some box offices are easier to reach than others, and there are two important points: (1) you usually cannot get any money back, and (2) you may likely have to pay the difference in price if the new date is now much more expensive, even if it is the exact same (or a worse) seat. Occasionally, you can get a refund, but this is very rare and should not be expected. Also, sometimes you will have to pay a small transaction fee to move your seat to a different seat even if for the same show time at the same price.

Because all sales are final, do be very careful and proofread everything before checking out.

8

WHERE TO STAY

There are pros and cons to staying in Times Square. If budget allows, Times Square can be the most convenient hotel location for trips with multiple shows. But it can also be very crowded, noisy, and very expensive during peak months. Staying a few subway stops away can save money at the expense of time, and the surrounding areas may be a bit more calm. For example, the West Village or Gramercy are nice areas that are still reasonably close but much more calm than Times Square. However, they might not be any less expensive than Times Square.

When an evening show is over, which might be as late as 11:00 PM, it is nice to just walk to your hotel room and not have to mess with the subway or a taxi. But if you do need to ride the subway, know that it will likely be full of other theatregoers, and I have found the subway to be relaxing and safe.

If I am seeing multiple shows in a day, which you can usually do on a Wednesday or Saturday and sometimes Sunday, I like that when staying in Times Square, I can easily go to my hotel room in between shows while also having time for dinner. And lastly, I do not have to worry about traffic or subway delays. I can leave my hotel less than an hour before curtain time and still get to the theatre plenty early.

When you are booking a hotel, just be sure to pay attention to the address, as there may be multiple hotels with the same name in New York City, as it is a big city. For example, there are multiple Courtyards, multiple Hilton Garden Inns, and multiple Hampton Inns in Times Square. I like to pull up my Maps app and confirm how far away the hotel is (using the address) from the theatre. You can use Sardi's restaurant as a reference point and see how far away your hotel is from Sardi's, as Sardi's is close to many theatre venues.

Also, be sure to check out the AAA discounted rate for the hotels you are considering, as the savings usually more than pays for the AAA annual membership fee. I almost always do the AAA rate, I do not pre-pay, and the cancellation requirement is usually three days or so prior to arrival. I generally do not recommend pre-paying for a nonrefundable hotel, since plans can change.

Do be sure to check your theatre location before booking the show, just to make sure it is actually in Manhattan, as sometimes you will get Internet suggestions for shows in Connecticut or Boston. Some Off-Broadway shows might be downtown and/or require a subway ride and not be walkable from your hotel, but it is fun to get out of Times Square. Just make your dinner plans close to your show venue, and make sure you allow enough time for travel. A bonus of making your dinner plans close to the theatre is that if you are unexpectedly running late (e.g., subway delay or traffic), you miss dinner instead of missing your show.

9

HOW TO DRESS

There is no official dress code for Broadway shows, but why not dress up? Many patrons choose to dress up, enjoy a nice dinner before the show, and then look nice at the performance. Do know that the theatre can be cold, especially in the summer, so be sure to bring a jacket or sweater. The hotter it is outside, the colder the theatre might be. For some shows, it can also be fun to dress according to the theme. For example, you will see a lot of green clothing at *Wicked.*

Opening Nights, which are typically invitation-only, are formal, but otherwise there is no firm dress code at most shows (*Masquerade* is a recent exception). I tend to dress based on the show and my mood that day. Sometimes I will wear a suit, and sometimes I will wear jeans and a sweater. I tend to more often dress up for an evening show than I do for a matinee. If you feel like it, break out the sequins and the fancy clothes, as going to a Broadway show is a special occasion! It is generally not possible to be overdressed. A sweatshirt with jeans is also fine. But I do always try to look nice when going to a show. I am not a fan of wearing sweats to a Broadway show, but it does happen. My favorite was a man in his I heart NYC tank top, sweatpants, and flip flops. But hey, perhaps this was a tourist who made a spontaneous last-minute decision to go enjoy a show—good for him! Do note that some restaurants and perhaps some theatre venues do not allow men to wear sleeveless shirts or flip flops. While this is generally ok for women, it is banned for men at nicer establishments. So guys, put on some sleeves and some real shoes if you are going to a restaurant that might require it. Also, remember the theatres can be very cold, especially in the summer.

Do take care to not wear anything that will interfere with the experience of the guests around you. For example, don't wear something so full and large that it will spill into the seats next to you. If you wear that witch's hat to *Wicked*, make sure you remove it during the show.

Two other considerations when figuring out your clothing is to know you may get caught in a downpour while in line to get in, and the subway underground can be very hot in the summer. I unfortunately do not have good solutions to these problems, but it is good to be aware of them.

10

DAY OF THE SHOW

Patrons who are sensitive to loud music may want to consider bringing hearing protection to musicals, as a few of the shows can be loud. You may find you rarely need to use them, as sound levels are usually appropriate in New York, but it can be nice to have them with you just in case a show is louder than you expect. There are special earplugs designed for concerts that do not muffle the sound as regular earplugs do. Visit previewnight.com and the Merch page for suggestions.

Bring cough drops and/or gum, just in case you get a tickle in your throat from the venue's HVAC system. It is also nice to have a cough drop to offer to a nearby patron who has a cough attack during the show. It is surprisingly common. A woman sitting behind me who was having a cough attack during a show must have thanked me ten times after I gave her a cough drop. If you have a cough attack that just won't stop, you actually should step out of the theatre until it is under control, unless you are at a show that does not allow re-entry if you step out. For example, *Just In Time* does not allow re-entry if you are seated on the floor and step out to use the restroom. This is due to the immersive nature of the show (you are effectively *in* the show when you have floor seats).

Consider bringing a mask in case you are seated next to someone who is noticeably ill. It happens. If you feel ill, please wear a mask (or don't go; the box office may be able to move your show date).

Bring a jacket or sweater, especially in summer months. It can be hard to regulate the venue's temperature, especially in older venues. It typically is hotter in the higher up seats and colder in the lower seats. The lower seats might need to be very cold in order to try and cool off the hot upper seats. This is especially an issue in the larger, historic regional theatres.

Do not take large bags or backpacks. Do not attempt to bring a camera or firearm inside. At most venues, you will need to pass through a metal detector and have your bag searched. Do not bring your luggage. Do not bring food or beverages! Check the venue's website for any additional restrictions.

If you plan to do stage door (discussed later in the book), you do not need to bring your own Sharpie. The cast members will almost always have their own Sharpie, and it will be a visible color that is compatible with that show's Playbill design (e.g., gold Sharpie if a black cover). You can bring a poster or other item for them to sign, as long as you can manage it during the show. In my experience, stuff you store under your seat gets stepped on. If the crowd is large, the actor may decline to sign anything other than your Playbill (more on this in a bit).

WHEN TO ARRIVE

Find out what time the doors open. There will generally be two different times. First is the time that you can enter the lobby. At small New York venues, this is sometimes just thirty minutes before curtain, but it can also be sixty to ninety minutes before if the venue has a lounge area where they are happy to sell you drinks and merchandise. Second, the "house" doors typically open twenty to thirty minutes before the show starts. The "house" refers to the auditorium.

Don't wait until the last minute to go to your seat. Many shows have a pre-show experience! A creative director will have your experience start the moment your ticket is scanned. Examples of shows where the show starts before the start time include *MJ the Musical*, *The Play That Goes Wrong*, and *Maybe Happy Ending*. Also, if people are in your seats, you need time to resolve the situation, as the show won't wait on you.

Once you get to your seat, chat with the folks around you, as everyone is excited to be there. Find out where they are from (might be from your hometown!), if they have seen the show before, and whatever else you are curious about. You might find out you are sitting next to the star's parents or spouse. Or you might find out you are sitting next to a lead from a different Broadway show, and they are there supporting their best friend in this show. They will then possibly give you some inside scoop about their show, and maybe you will go support your seat neighbor the next time they are on stage! For example, I sat next to a national tour performer on her day off when we were both at the play, *Purpose*, and several months later, she unexpectedly made her Broadway debut! She was kind enough to add my name to "the list" at Stage Door, so I was able to bypass the crowd and say hi after the show (more on Stage Door in a bit).

A word about seat numbers if you have multiple tickets: do not panic if they are not consecutive. Some theatres do odd numbers on one side of the house and even numbers on the other side of the house. So seats two and four may indeed be next to each other.

Many shows have door holds if you are late, so do not be late! A door hold means that once the show starts, you are not allowed to enter until that scene is over. This may be ten minutes or more. In the case of *Disney's The Lion King*, if you are late, you will miss the best scene of the entire show and perhaps one of the best scenes ever in musical theatre!

A good rule of thumb is to arrive forty to sixty minutes early at a Broadway show and thirty minutes early at an Off-Broadway show. Restroom lines will be very long and will get longer closer to the start of the show. Most people arrive at the last minute, so you can avoid some of the crowd by arriving early.

FOOD AND BEVERAGE CONSIDERATIONS

Many of us learn the hard way not to overeat before a show. It can be very uncomfortable to sit for two to three hours with an overly full stomach. Similarly, watch how much you drink, including water, as especially women may not be able to get through the long restroom line during intermission, which is typically only fifteen minutes long.

WHERE TO EAT BEFORE THE SHOW

One of my favorite places to dine before a show is Sardi's. The location is also excellent, as it is close to many Broadway theatres. There are enough good items on the menu that you can have something different each time. Be sure to be observant while you are there, as you may notice stars in the house. If you do, please respect their privacy. Do not approach stars while they are having dinner. Sardi's has both a downstairs and upstairs dining area, as well as an upstairs bar.

If you are looking for a restaurant reasonably close to your theatre, there are also many good choices on 9th Avenue, which is slightly less chaotic than the very busy 7th Avenue. In general, walking on 9th Avenue is a great tip to avoid the large crowds on Broadway and on 7th and 8th Avenues. Many of the dining options on 9th Avenue are also open late.

Just let your server know you are going to a show, and almost all restaurants in midtown are very skilled at getting a rush of pre-show diners in and out in a timely manner. Make reservations if you are in town during a peak tourism month.

SUBWAY VS. RIDE SHARE VS. TAXI

Almost always, the subway is going to be your best bet. Traffic is usually at a standstill near the theatres, and the subway is generally faster. The negatives of the subway are that it can be very hot underground in the summer while waiting for the subway (on the subway is generally comfortable), and you could get caught in a downpour walking from the subway to the theatre. Just know that if you choose the car route, you will need to leave very, very early.

The subways in New York City are generally safe, including after a show. As always, just be aware of your surroundings. Put your wallet and phone in your front pocket, not your back pocket. If you plan to utilize taxis, check out the Curb app. The Curb app works like Lyft or Uber but with official Yellow Cab taxis. According to nyc.gov, "Yellow Cab Taxicabs are the only vehicles that have the right to pick up street-hailing and prearranged passengers anywhere in New York City."

If you have an iPhone, go to *Settings -> Wallet & Apple Pay* and set up "Express Transit Card" under Transit Cards. This will allow you to simply tap your phone as your payment method for the subway. If you have an Apple Watch, you can also set this up on your Watch and then only need to raise your wrist in order to pay.

I tend to prefer flying to JFK, but I suggest prioritizing whichever airport provides you with a direct flight.

If you are traveling from JFK to Manhattan, consider the

Long Island Rail Road (LIRR), as it can sometimes be much faster and superior to the subway, while only costing slightly more. You first take the JFK AirTrain to Jamaica Station, and then you transfer to the LIRR and head to Penn Station. You may find it a bit confusing the first few times you try to figure out what train and what track, so you may need to allow for some extra time for this. But it can be significantly faster than the subway, and the train is a fun experience. In reverse, you go to Penn Station and then take the LIRR to Jamaica Station. Then you take the AirTrain from Jamaica Station to your JFK terminal.

The JFK AirTrain can get very crowded, so during peak travel periods, you might just want to do a taxi, especially if you have a lot of luggage. When you are returning to the airport, it is important to know ahead of time what terminal you need to go to, as they are not connected after security. Getting off at the wrong terminal would be a major mistake, so this is an important tip for your return trip.

You may be approached by a driver asking you if you need a ride. It is generally best to not accept these solicitations, as these drivers can possibly be unlicensed, uninsured, and/or may possibly charge you a rate higher than the regulated rate. Be cautious of solicitors who hang out near the ground transportation lines. Similarly, don't personally pay someone for a subway pass, train ticket, or taxi fare.

11

AT THE SHOW

RESTROOMS

Depending on the size of the venue, you may experience several different types of restrooms, including gender labeled restrooms, all-gender restrooms, family restrooms, and accessible restrooms. A gender labeled restroom is a traditional restroom that typically indicates "Men" or "Women," and most theatres encourage patrons to use the restroom they feel most comfortable in. An all-gender restroom is a restroom that ideally has fully enclosed closets for each stall and possibly has shared hand-washing areas. A family restroom is a small private restroom where a caregiver can provide assistance. An accessible restroom has added features for physically disabled patrons.

When possible, do not use the accessible restroom unless you need it, since there may only be one or two of these. Similarly, if you see someone using an accessible restroom who in your judgment does not need it, please remember many disabilities are invisible, and it is not your place to judge or to enforce the restroom policies.

If unclear where to go, you can ask an usher. You might also observe some women using the labeled men's restroom, as the lines for the labeled women's restroom can be unreasonably long. I actually overheard a man complain to an usher one time about an all-gender restroom, "I don't want to see women squatting over the urinals!" No, don't worry, that's never going to happen. Women have been using the men's restroom when lines are unreasonably long since the beginning of time; this is nothing new.

If you are seeing a long show, it is a good idea before the show to determine which restroom is the closest to your seat, so at intermission, you know the fastest and most direct route to the restroom. The restroom lines will get long five to ten minutes before the show starts and again at intermission. Therefore, it is a good idea to use the restroom about fifteen minutes before the show starts. Restrooms at intermission are discussed below.

YOUR PROGRAM

In New York City, your show program, frequently a Playbill® program, is included in your ticket price and does not need to be purchased separately. This program will tell you about the cast, including their biographies, and will also have advertisements about other shows and theatre-related content. Your program may have a paper insert notifying you of some cast changes at your performance. This usually indicates one or more actors have "called out" for your performance, perhaps due to illness, and a standby or understudy is filling in. Fear not, the understudies in New York City are outstanding and might be just as good as the usual performer. You definitely want to see a healthy understudy and not a sick performer. However, if the major star of the show is out, you can often get a refund if the actor's name is "above the title."

ETIQUETTE

If you remember nothing else, please remember these rules:

1. No talking during the show. Save your thoughts for after the show.
2. No singing along at a musical, except for rare instances where the cast tells you to (for that song only).
3. No candy or food wrappers, even if allowed by the venue.
4. No eating during the performance, even if allowed by the venue.
5. No phones out during the performance, ever, except possibly during closing bows (if allowed).
6. Completely power down your phone and smart watch.
7. If you are coughing a lot, exit until it is under control (unless your show has a no re-entry policy).

FIRST, let's talk about the talking. One would think this is common sense, as people do not even like this during a movie. But it happens a lot. The reason this is extra important at a play or musical is not only because you are disturbing everyone around you, but also because the cast can hear you. Do not be that person who causes an actor to forget a line.

The only acceptable scenario where it is ok to talk is if you notice a fire or other actual emergency. If there is no emergency, do not talk. At the same time, do not shush someone who is talking, for three reasons: (1) it most likely will not work, as most people who talk during a show continue to talk even after being shushed, (2) your "shhhh" will likely be louder than that person's talking, causing YOU to disturb the cast and everyone around you, and (3) the rude person who cannot be quiet may escalate the situation and make matters much worse. This is surprisingly common. Instead, report the talking to the usher during intermission, and the usher can provide a reminder. It is the venue's job, not your job, to provide an acceptable environment.

Next, singing along at a musical is a common mistake, especially since many find it to be acceptable behavior at a concert. At a musical, it is unacceptable behavior. People paid good money to hear the Broadway performers sing. No matter how good you think you are, they did not pay to hear you sing, and you are now interfering with their experience. An exception is if the cast invites you to sing along.

Your phone or any device that lights up should never be in use during the show. The light from the screen will distract everyone around you. While this is common practice at a concert, it is never ok to have your phone out during a play or musical while the performance is underway. A possible exception is taking pictures or video during the closing bows, after the performance is over, if allowed.

It is best to completely power down your phone and smart watch, because too many features override the silent mode. These include alarms, Amber Alerts, and Find My Phone features. Also, nobody wants to hear the loud buzzing from vibrate mode.

I was at a musical one time when the loud Find My Phone alert kept continuously playing over and over in the audience. What had happened was a man's iPhone was in his wife's purse (I do not know why), she went to the show, he did not, and he then was later trying to locate his phone. So he kept doing Find My Phone over and over again. Even after she silenced it, he would make it beep again. This went on for several minutes, and the patron was obviously devastated. She had silenced her phone as instructed. Adding to her embarrassment, she was a personal guest of one of the cast members! The only way to avoid this is to completely power down the phone.

Similarly, in December 2025, Apple started promoting a new feature where Reminders can automatically create Alarms that override silent mode. Do you see the problem?

Nobody plans for the phone to make noise, so again, just power it completely down. Think of the battery you will save. Remember to power it back down again after intermission.

While it is fine to munch away on that popcorn and candy at a movie theater, it is not ok at a play or musical. Candy wrappers are noisy not only for everyone around you but also for the cast. My favorite example was patrons who smuggled in pizza to a show. The cast finally had to comment, "we can smell your food!" Some venues are now allowing noisy candy wrappers into their venues as a way to increase revenues, but this is very disruptive to the cast. Even if the venue has decided to enable the rudeness, do not be the person who opens a candy wrapper or eats food during a show. The noise and smell are a distraction. You will survive if you go three hours without any candy. Eat before the show, during intermission, and/or after the show, but do not eat during the performance.

We have all been there where you get a tickle in your throat and cannot stop coughing. Sometimes it is due to the venue's HVAC system. Coughing is very loud and distracting to the cast and audience. If this happens to you sometimes, be sure to have cough drops or gum in your pocket. Just remember to open that cough drop wrapper very quietly! If you are coughing more than a couple of times, exit the auditorium until you get the coughing under control, unless you are at a show that has a no re-entry policy.

If you are sitting in the front row of loge, mezzanine, or balcony, do not put anything on the ledge in front of you. There are primarily two reasons: (1) the item could fall and hit a patron down below in the head, or (2) the item could potentially catch on fire if it touches the nearby lighting, which can be very hot. If you do put something on the ledge, expect to get scolded by an usher fairly quickly, as they are instructed to prioritize enforcing this safety rule.

If someone is trying to enter or exit your row, please stand to let them pass. The aisleways are tight, and you do not want to have your feet stepped on. You also don't want to trip the person.

As previously mentioned, talk to your seat neighbors before the show and during intermission. They are interesting people! I met an ICU nurse from London who flew in for one night only just to see Hugh Jackman, I have met the directors of numerous shows, and I have gotten great restaurant tips and other show tips. Often, I find out that my seat neighbors and I are seeing additional shows together in the future.

At a musical, cheer and applaud loudly after each song finishes! Just try to wait until the song is actually over. The cast works hard and appreciates the recognition. It is rare to give a standing ovation in the middle of a show after a song, but it can happen, especially at special performances. For example, on December 15, 2025, MCC Theatre hosted a benefit concert of *The Bridges of Madison County* at Carnegie Hall, and the Original Broadway Cast performed. Both Kelli O'Hara and Steven Pasquale each received a standing ovation after powerful solo performances. This is also happening sometimes at *Ragtime* at Lincoln Center Theater, and as previously mentioned, it happened at *Gypsy* the night before the Tony Awards in June 2025.

During closing bows, some will argue the etiquette is actually to wait to stand until the leads finally come out. But this is rarely followed, and many people stand right away. There is really no right or wrong answer, as deciding to do a standing ovation is a personal decision. My rule of thumb is I often wait for the leads unless there is a supporting actor I really liked, or I will go ahead and stand if I can no longer see, due to everyone else standing. If people in front of me stand, I go ahead and stand. Of course, do not judge those around you who do not stand, especially since they might be unable to stand.

RUNNING LATE

If you are late to a show, you likely will not be allowed in until a designated break in the story where you will be (slightly) less disruptive to the cast and to the rest of the audience. This period of time where you have to wait before being allowed to take your seat is referred to as a "door hold."

Some shows may refuse late seating ever, meaning you miss the show. Other shows may give away your seats to patrons on a standby list.

If you tend to run late, my suggestion is to target being at the theatre sixty minutes before the scheduled start time, and schedule your nearby dinner to be an additional sixty to ninety minutes earlier. It is disruptive and rude to the cast and to the audience to be late.

12

INTERMISSION RESTROOM STRATEGY

A s soon as the lights come up, GO! Now don't step on anyone, and do not push. But it is common for there to be a three-to-five-second delay before people stand up after the lights come on. They are trying to figure out if it is indeed intermission, so they are waiting to see what everyone else around them is going to do. But every second counts when it comes to the intermission restroom line, and because you bought this book, you know with 100% certainty that when the house lights come up, it is indeed intermission, and you need to make a run for it (not literally), especially if you are a woman.

I do not recommend trying to leave before the lights come up, as this is potentially dangerous, and it is rude to those around you. Only do this if you are about to have an accident. But once those lights come up, do get going. This is when having an aisle seat is a nice perk. Now if your show is over and does not have an intermission, then this advice does not apply. The goal here is to get back to Act 2 before it starts, but you can slow down if the show is actually over.

A side note is it is a good idea to ask your usher for the run time (or look it up), because it is nice to know if your show is ninety minutes with no intermission or two hours and forty-five minutes with a ninety-minute first act. I have sadly seen people leave and go home after a long Act 1, as they mistakenly thought the show was over.

At the start of intermission, it is perfectly fine to say, "sorry, excuse me, sorry" as you walk past your seat neighbors who are still just sitting there trying to decide what to do. Every second counts, and you shouldn't miss the start of Act 2 just because they didn't read this book.

If you have a child with you, hold their hand and pull them along with you. Do exit with urgency. This is your window and can mean the difference between getting back to your seat in time, versus waiting for a curtain hold at the start of Act 2. Even five to ten seconds can equal five to ten minutes, and you only have fifteen minutes total. This is especially important for women and increasingly important for men in venues that have removed urinals in favor of all-gender restrooms exclusively.

I will stop short of advising you to run to the restroom, as this increases the chances of injury to you and others, but it is not uncommon to see women running at intermission. The lines really are that bad, but absolutely do not run, push, or shove, and be especially cautious near stairs.

Be mindful of disabled patrons, elderly patrons, and children. I attended a show soon after eye surgery, and I was wearing an eye patch, dark sunglasses, and I was using a cane, since I had zero peripheral vision on one side of my body. I was absolutely shocked and horrified how many people—theatre people!—slammed into me, pushed me, bumped me, and taught me new empathy for theatre patrons with disabilities. I chatted about this with another patron who was using a cane, and he validated that he is pushed and shoved all the time. Please be aware of your surroundings and those around you in the crowded theatre at all times, not just when you are hurrying to the restroom.

If you do not make it back to your seat in time and find yourself returning to your seat after Act 2 has already started, please be courteous not just to your fellow audience members but also to the cast. The cast likely cannot see you when the house lights are down, but they can hear you! If you have children with you, remind them to be very quiet before you re-enter the house.

After intermission, turn your phone and smart watch back off. Turn them all the way off, not just silenced.

13

AFTER THE SHOW

I t is rude and bad etiquette to leave your seat before the lights come up and before the curtain has come back down (or until the cast has left the stage, if there is no curtain). Take this time to applaud and cheer the cast for their hard work.

The cast can now see you, and it is very disrespectful for you to rush out before they have left the stage. They have just given you hours of joy, and now it's your turn to pay it back with applause and cheers.

Once the lights are up and the final bows are done, this is the time to exit. Again, be mindful of disabled and elderly patrons.

STAGE DOOR

After the show, many fans will line up at the stage door to hope to meet some of the cast members, get their autographs, and possibly get a picture together. There is no expectation cast members will come out, so this is a special treat and not an entitlement. It is less likely cast members will come out after a matinee on a two-show day, as they need to eat and rest up for their second show that day.

At Broadway theatres, the stage door experience is fairly organized with security personnel keeping it all under control. At Off-Broadway venues, it can sometimes be a bit chaotic if there is a big star, as these venues—especially if located downtown and not midtown—might have zero stage door management.

As you are exiting the show, you can ask an usher, "which way is the stage door?" and you will be told generally which way to go (you usually just need to know whether to go left or right once you are outside). At most venues, it is obvious, and you will see the crowd. At a few theatres, the stage door might actually be one block away at the rear of the building. When it's less obvious, sometimes you will have a smaller crowd, as not everyone knows how to find the stage door and didn't think to ask an usher.

Be sure to line up behind the barrier, because if you block a path, you will be moved. Sometimes, you can get lucky and be right up against the barrier, pretty much guaranteeing autographs as long as some cast members come out. If the crowd is already there, see if you can be immediately behind and in between two people, where you could envision sticking your arm holding your Playbill in between the two people in front of you. If you hold your Playbill out, the actor will sign it. The person in front of you who just got their Playbill signed will usually cooperate and let you stick in your arm. Cast members will typically acknowledge someone immediately behind the front row of fans, but they might not sign Playbills of folks farther back. They want to get through everyone that is along the barrier and then go home to eat and sleep!

Sometimes cast members will come out and go straight to a car without stopping to sign Playbills. And then you will sometimes hear rude, entitled fans boo or comment that they paid good money to meet the cast. No. The ticket is for the show. Please be respectful of the actor's choice. They might be exhausted, feeling sick, or just trying to get to some dinner plans. Again, there should be no expectation of them doing a meet and greet. It is a favor and a special treat.

If a performer does stop to sign your Playbill and possibly take a selfie with you, be courteous to the performer and other fans and limit your engagement. You might want to chat with the performer for ten or more minutes, but five to ten seconds would be more appropriate.

You should NEVER follow a performer after they leave the venue. You should also not engage with a performer once they have left the stage door area and are trying to go home.

Once security tells you, "that's it!" it is time to leave. It doesn't matter if you correctly predict the big star will exit the stage door ten minutes later, after Security clears the crowd, because obviously, that actor is wanting to leave without fan interaction after this performance for whatever reason. Be respectful, and leave when it's time to leave. The performer wants to go home but now perhaps cannot leave the building until you stop loitering outside the door.

When a performer is signing your Playbill, if you politely ask, "can I please take a quick picture?" they will almost always say yes. Just be quick, as other fans are waiting. If the crowd is very large, they will sometimes say no to doing anything more than signing your Playbill. I suggest being selective and only taking photos with your favorites. Get everyone's signature on your Playbill, as that is fast, but photos take longer.

Stage Door is a privilege that is currently at risk, due to inappropriate stalker-like behavior by just a few individuals who then ruin it for all. So please be respectful and follow these etiquette tips, so that everyone can have a fun and safe experience.

14

CLOSING

Live theatre relies on word of mouth, so DO post on social media, share your pictures, and tell all your friends about the show! If you got a great pic of your favorite cast member, tag the actor, and you might get a like back!

If you found this book to be helpful, please also spread the word about this book! Information about this book is available at broadwayforbeginners.com. If you found anything in this book boring or confusing, or if you have any feedback at all, please use the contact form at previewnightpress.com to let us know, so we can consider incorporating your feedback into a possible future edition.

While this book contains a lot of information to digest, remember that at the end of the day, there is really no wrong choice in which show(s) you select—unless you decide to see zero shows. If you pick your second choice show over your first choice show, chances are you will have an incredible time. If you decide not to see one specific show this trip, and then it unexpectedly closes a week after you leave town, that is just the way it goes! It is not possible to see every show. Consider prioritizing a show that has its original cast, especially if it includes a big star. Most stars are only in the show for a limited period of time.

Consider prioritizing a show you really want to see that might be closing soon. If you know that it would be smarter to see a new show with its original cast that is closing soon (yes, you should pick this one if it has good reviews), but you just really, really want to see *Hamilton* or *Wicked* or *Lion King* in New York and don't know when you will get back to town, then do it! These productions on Broadway are indeed better than their national tours (but their national tour productions are also very good).

If you cannot decide between two shows, but one of them has incredible seats available while the other does not, pick the one with the great seats.

If you know the show you want but can't decide whether you should spend that extra hundred dollars for a better seat, do it if your budget allows. Your time is valuable, and why not have the best possible experience? On the flip side, you will still likely have a good time no matter where your seat is.

If you cannot decide between two shows where one of them is one you really, really want to see but it is so expensive, while the other one is less exciting but a fraction of the price, know you will have a good time at either one! Sometimes, a show with a higher price is worth it, but there are also times the ticket price is just too high. The good news is there is no wrong choice.

Do plan ahead if it is a show you really, really want to see, in case it becomes sold out.

Thank you so much for reading this book! If you found this book helpful, please consider sharing on social media and/or posting a review, so others can also discover these tips. Enjoy your shows!

ABOUT THE AUTHOR

Brian Guy is an Off-Broadway co-producer, author, and theatre enthusiast. His books include *The Best of Broadway (and Beyond): A 2026 Review of Last Year's Standout Shows.*

Brian is co-founder of Neurodiversity Allies, a nonprofit organization advocating for sensory accessibility in theatre.

He is passionate about helping new and occasional theatregoers feel confident, informed, and welcome. Brian resides on Bainbridge Island in Washington State.

instagram.com/brianguytheatre

facebook.com/brianguytheatre

ALSO BY BRIAN GUY

The Best of Broadway (and Beyond): A 2026 Review of Last Year's
Standout Shows

PREVIEW NIGHT PRESS

An imprint of Preview Night, LLC

previewnightpress.com